AF335416

LAWRENCE CLARK POWELL. *Photograph by Cynthia Farah.*

"Next to Mother's Milk..."

an Engelhard Lecture on the Book
presented by
LAWRENCE CLARK POWELL
at the Library of Congress
on Tuesday, April 8, 1986

LIBRARY OF CONGRESS
WASHINGTON
1987

The Center for the Book Viewpoint Series, no. 17

Library of Congress Cataloging-in-Publication Data

Powell, Lawrence Clark, 1906–
"Next to mother's milk—".

(The Center for the Book viewpoint series ; 17)
Includes bibliographical references.
1. Books and reading—United States. 2. Powell, Lawrence Clark, 1906– —Books and reading. 3. Authors, American—20th century—Biography. 4. Librarians—United States—Biography. I. Title. II. Title: Engelhard lecture on the book. III. Series.
Z1003.2.P69 1987 028'.9'0973 87–4160
ISBN 0–8444–0551–5

This booklet is printed on acid-free paper.

Preface

Lawrence Clark Powell is perhaps the country's quintessential bookman and bibliophile, so his lecture at the Library of Congress on April 8, 1986, was a special occasion for the sponsor, the Center for the Book in the Library of Congress. Powell's fundamental belief in the power of books to educate focuses our attention on the best characteristics of the book: its accessibility and its capability of adapting to the needs of each reader. For decades his writings have inspired hundreds of students, including myself, to seek careers in the world of books. His firm beliefs, his personal example, and his infectious love of collecting, reading, and even giving away books, make Larry Powell one of the spiritual fathers of the Center for the Book.

No one can predict what influence a book may have, as Larry Powell's indirect influence on my own career attests. In 1961 I had not heard of him but accidentally came across his *Books in My Baggage,* a collection of essays published the previous year. I was capitivated by the essays, but also learned from the description of the author on the dust jacket that there actually were places called professional library schools! I soon found my way to one, and eventually to the Library of Congress.

Powell is a hard character to characterize. He was born in Washington, D.C., in 1906. One of the highlights of his return in 1986 was a visit to his childhood home at 1867 Park Road, N.W. He grew up in southern California and made his professional career there, and he will always be closely associated with the University of California at Los Angeles. He was University Librarian there from 1944 to 1961 and founding Dean of the Graduate School of Library and Information Science, holding that position from 1960 to 1966. He also is known as a citizen of the Great American Southwest, which he has written about and where he now lives with his wife Fay. The large audience that came to hear Larry Powell on April 8 knew him best from his writings on books, but he is also a novelist and a writer of essays about music, the landscape, poetry, and even administration. The breadth of his interests is documented in his autobiography, published by Bowker and the Scarecrow Press in two volumes thus far: *Fortune & Friendship* (1968) and *Life Goes On: Twenty More Years of Fortune and Friendship* (1986).

The Center for the Book in the Library of Congress was established by law in 1977 to stimulate public interest in books, reading, and the printed word. Its program is supported primarily by private contributions from individuals and corporations. The Center is grateful to Mrs. Charles W. Engelhard for a donation that made Lawrence Clark Powell's presentation possible and which enables us, through this publication, to share his enthusiasm with a wide audience.

John Y. Cole
Director
The Center for the Book

"Next to Mother's Milk..."

"Next to mother's milk...."

Meaning what? Who would dare come to the Library of Congress to talk about anything other than books? Or, to talk about books not as precious objects to be handled with gloves but rather as utilitarian objects, sometimes even to be mishandled and often to be marked up—and always to be read—about books as preservers and transmitters of what distinguishes us from the other animals.

We are here because we believe in the power of books to educate—a belief propagated through the Center for the Book by the Librarian of Congress, in the great tradition that leads back to the founding fathers, notably Thomas Jefferson. Today our national library is more than ever a radiating center for this best way to package and disseminate what is truly "next to mother's milk the best food." By this I mean books in whatever form they may take. As leaders in this work I salute Daniel Boorstin, John Cole, and their colleagues.

How did I come to choose this title? The answer goes back sixty-two years to when Ward Ritchie (who also spoke here last fall) * and I came as freshmen to Occidental College, a small liberal arts school on the borders

* Ward Ritchie's lecture, delivered at the Library of Congress on October 2, 1985, will be published as *Fine Printing: The Los Angeles Tradition* (Washington: Library of Congress, in press).

of Los Angeles and Pasadena. He and I had grown up together in South Pasadena, and this was our first venture into the world. It was the first stop on a journey we have been taking together ever since, always with books as our bread and butter—he as artist and printer and I as librarian, teacher, and writer.

I left high school in 1924, inspired by a teacher of history whose habit of chewing his words before uttering them led us to call him Bunny Wilson. His passion for history and geography convinced me to follow him to a similar teaching career. He emphasized the influence of the land on history, and I was ready.

Ever impressionable and restless from birth, I made my first transcontinental journey at age four months, from Washington, D.C., to Southern California, where I was to grow up. My horticulturist father, a protégé of Cornell's great Liberty Hyde Bailey, was then in the Bureau of Plant Industry of the Department of Agriculture, and he had been sent as head of a team of fellow scientists to solve a problem affecting the Southland's lucrative citrus industry. The loss by decay of fruit in transit to the eastern markets was costing the growers millions of dollars. Five winters of fieldwork in the groves, packinghouses, and laboratory, from 1903 to 1908, proved that the decay was due to bruises and punctures caused by rough picking and packing. The villain was *penicillum glaucum*—blue mold.

My father's published monograph revolutionized the handling of fruit, and it resulted in his being named to head the great Sunkist cooperative. And so in the last days of 1910 we moved permanently to the Golden Land. Those great crossings by train each winter from 1906 were harbingers of a life of travel in which the Book became my passport, honored the world over from Aberystwyth to Zagreb.

In September 1924, Ward Ritchie and I found ourselves in the back row of a small class in comparative literature, drawn by the reputation of the instructor, the young Carlyle Ferren MacIntyre, not long back from graduate work in Germany, where he had taken his doctorate at the University of Marburg with a dissertation on color in Rossetti's poetry. Something more than that achievement had given him the exotic name he had on the campus of what was then a religion-oriented school where daily chapel was compulsory.

MacIntyre was a bohemian, said to make his own wine and beer (this was during Prohibition) and also to tempt coeds off campus by writing alluring love lyrics. How the college came to hire him and how he lasted only four years is another story.

Mac would come to campus driving a topless Pierce Arrow roadster, abandon it in a no-parking zone, and rush in to class as the bell rang, throwing down briefcase and black Stetson, glaring at the class and growling,

"Who wants to be the first to talk? No one? Well then, my little Christians, wake up and listen to me."

What followed then was an hour of wide-awake intellectual discussion new to us, who were mostly from conservative middle-class homes. Through literature he sought to replace our narrow view of religion with a world view of a common culture that encompassed China, India, Persia, Greece, Europe, and the New World. Of course it was far over our heads, to be reached for and possibly grasped only with curiosity and motivation, with which he sought passionately to imbue us.

Thus our cultural barriers were battered down by that fierce chieftain of Clan MacIntyre. He sent us reading to Li Po, Omar Khayam, Meleager, and Sappho, and on to Villon, Herrick, Heine, Housman, and Hardy, and also to the philosopher-poets Confucius, Zoroaster, Sophocles, Dante, Milton, and Goethe. We were exposed for the first time to teaching both merciless and kind. We learned that it was best to duel with him, lest we be struck down and made foolish. The unresponsive were simply left behind in the rush of that semester, which ended too soon.

His favorite target was the inadequate college library. Form your own library, he urged; go downtown and ransack the bookshops: Dawson's and Louis Epstein's. Jake Zeitlin had not yet arrived from Texas to set up his snailshell of a shop, destined to become the calm heart of the whirlwind which struck the country a few years later to herald the Depression.

On the first day of class, MacIntyre sent us to a list he had posted in the college library which gave the reading we would be held responsible for at the end of the semester. He had temporarily deposited there his own copies of the recommended works. That list was headed by these words: "Books, next to mother's milk the best food." There were other quotations, from Chaucer on down. As I recall, only that first quotation bore no attribution. I confess never having sought beyond Bartlett and Holbrook Jackson. Was it by MacIntyre himself?

After that class in comparative literature, I was lost to history and geography. Only years later did I find my way back in writing about California and the Southwest. Ritchie and I were not completely unprepared for the mauling we received. He and I and the late William A. Jackson of the Houghton Library had grown up in the Carnegie Library of South Pasadena where Librarian Nellie Keith said Yes when our teachers said No.

The other great influence in my life was my mother, who gave me books from the beginning: books of the two Stevensons, Burton E. and RLS, Grimms' Fairy Tales, and a set of the Book of Knowledge. Only that copy of the *Home Book of Verse* has survived, the fattest of all the books I have ever owned, and one of the most nourishing and useful, even to serving as a doorstop when the wind sweeps over the desert. The disappearance of my Jessie Wilcox Smith-illustrated *Child's Garden of Verses* didn't matter, as I knew my favorites by heart.

My father also gave me books. One was prophetic: *Through the Grand Canyon from Wyoming to Mexico,* today the cornerstone of a working collection on the Southwest. Incidentally, we are *not* descended from that most celebrated Powell, Maj. John Wesley, the first to run the Grand Canyon. He was a Methodist; we were Quakers.

My parents also gave books to each other. At Christmas 1904 my mother gave my father a copy of *Leaves of Grass.* When he died in 1922 at fifty, that book became hers. A decade later, I was in France for graduate study at the University of Dijon (much to MacIntyre's disgust, I having been expected to go as he did to Germany). One of my thesis topics there was Whitman's perception of the Pacific Coast—which, incidentally, he never saw. Then my mother sent me that copy. I still have it, bearing her underlinings, made during a time of emotional turmoil in her own life.

What books did my father give her? In 1900 it was a set of the Wheatley edition of Pepys's Diary, which became her second Bible as she went on to read and collect Pepys in earnest when, after moving to Southern California and being attracted to what was then known as New Thought, she grew convinced that her husband was the reincarnation of Pepys. It *is* true that both men had unusual scientific curiosity and administrative ability, as well as a love of dancing and the fair sex. I teased her once by giving her a book about Pepys's wife, Elizabeth St. Michel, inscribed to Gertrude Powell Pepys from Lawrence Powell Pepys.

Alas, she did not live to enjoy the definitive edition of the Diary by William Mathews and Robert Latham. With my UCLA colleague, the late Will Mathews, I shared an interest in both Pepys and baseball. From my first sight of the manuscript in Magdalen College, Cambridge, I was convinced that it had been written from notes, sometimes a week or more after the events—and I said so in my *Alchemy of Books* (1954). This was confirmed by Mathews's subsequent research.

During those boyhood years my father sometimes brought home for dinner a friend who wrote children's books. Whenever he came he brought a copy of his newest book, inscribed to us three boys; and after he left, there ensued a tussle for who got to read it first. Thus was accumulated our own set of the Oz books. Where are they now? Long since read to pieces.

Such then are some of the books and influences which shaped my life. The Depression was another. It forced me to abandon my intention to teach literature and to free-lance as a writer. There were no jobs, no sales. That tough Scot Ritchie made it through by narrowing his sights, and by talent and hard work. Sad to say, MacIntyre was fired successively by Occidental, UCLA, and Berkeley. The cause was always the same: an unconventional personal life and outspoken contempt for lazy colleagues and overactive administrators.

He never forgave or forgot. When he laid his termination at UCLA to a powerful member of his department, he took revenge on her in a poem called "The Old Red Camel." His publisher stood by him in the face of a threatened libel suit. After he was transferred to Berkeley, the support of August Frugé, longtime director of the University of California Press, resulted in Mac's successful translations of Goethe, Georg, Rilke, Baudelaire, Verlaine, and Corbière. Finally, during long residence in Paris he became the best-known American expatriate since Hemingway and Stein. Royalties and the devotion of his wife Marian solaced his final years before he was felled by a stroke and died in 1967 at age seventy-six. Long before that, I had begun to amass his archive at UCLA, where it now awaits his editor and biographer.

What initially got me through the Depression was a high school course in stenography. When Jake Zeitlin needed someone to take dictation and type—and also dress the shop window, wrap, sell, and deliver—I got the job. Jake taught me all that and more as he became another of the few decisive people in my life. During those two and a half years with him I did everything but grow rich. Then it was either go into the book business for myself or become a librarian and renounce all hope of riches and worldly advancement. I chose the latter, and with Fay and our two little sons I went off to Berkeley for a further year of study.

Those learning years with Jake prepared me to be a spokesman for better understanding between the antiquarian booktrade and research libraries. My first Guggenheim fellowship in 1950 enabled me to pursue this effort in Great Britain, which also resulted in some of UCLA's finest coups: the Ogden, Sadleir, and Foot collections. I confess to having been too absorbed that year in collecting Lawrence Durrell to perceive the emerging genius of the late Philip Larkin.

As president of the Bibliographical Society of America in 1954-56, I persuaded the council to elect its first member from the antiquarian booktrade: the late Frances Hamill. Regional meetings were held in Ann Arbor, Chicago, San Marino, and Washington. At that last meeting, papers were given by Millicent Sowerby on Jefferson's library and by Sol Malkin on the present state of bibliography. Those who heard Sol that day in the Elizabethan theater of the Folger Library, lubricating his talk with sips of brandy, will never forget the occasion. Dear Sol, may there be only sleepers where you have gone!

My first indirect connection with the Library of

Congress came in 1910 through my mother, when she was shown through the still-new Jefferson Building by Librarian Herbert Putnam, a friend of her cousin. Years later the tie was strengthened when in 1939 Archibald MacLeish was nominated to the Librarianship by FDR, and the American Library Association howled in official protest. I was a junior librarian then at UCLA, attending my first ALA conference at San Francisco.

MacLeish's poems had been part of my essential baggage during student years abroad. I used them once in an argument with a Turkish poet and law student who claimed that American poetry began and ended with Whitman. I accepted only the first part of that claim, and made him listen to MacLeish's "You, Andrew Marvell," with its luminous lines:

> And here face down beneath the sun
>   And here upon earth's noonward height
> To feel the always coming on
>   The always rising of the night.

Many years passed before I met that dogmatic Turk again. By then he had become rector of the University of Istanbul. As director of the UCLA library, I had the privilege of showing him around campus, each amused by how the other's life had turned out.

At that general session of the ALA, I brashly spoke in support of the MacLeish nomination, declaring that librarians would benefit from a closer association with literature. My library school dean did not agree. "Sit down, you damn fool," he hissed, "before you ruin your career." What career, I thought, my salary having reached $145 a month and no relief in sight.

A few years later when it had risen all of $10 a month, President Roosevelt's confirmed choice came to campus as Charter Day speaker. Among my bibliographical assignments was that of arranging the library's public exhibits. I prepared a display of the books of Rilke, Yeats, and MacLeish and persuaded my chief to bring the poet-librarian by to see it. He had only a moment to spare. Although eager to talk books with him, I remained respectfully unobtrusive. In moving on, he only said to me, "You do me great honor."

Years later near the end of MacLeish's long and useful life, I asked Ward Ritchie and Richard Hoffman to print a booklet and a broadside of another of my favorites of his poems, "On the Beaches of the Moon." Our men had landed there, and the poet's vision of fifty years earlier had come true:

> Only in the cloudless sky
>   Moves by day the sun; by night
> Slow among the stars the white
>   Silence of the Earth goes by

In acknowledging the copies sent him, the poet corrected

himself, saying that in the *Apollo* photographs the earth appeared blue not white!

There were other ties with the Library of Congress when I became a member of the advisory committee of the Association of Research Libraries, which of course included the Library of Congress, the greatest of all. Thus I came to know Luther Evans, Verner Clapp, David Mearns, Lewis Hanke, Herman Henkle, Fred Wagman, Lucille Morsch, and Freddie Goff. A lasting tie is with John Charles Finzi, once a student clerk on my staff. Our peerless Oscar Wilde collection needed its manuscripts cataloged. Finzi did it so well that the University of California Press published his catalog as *Oscar Wilde and His Literary Circle*. I am happy also to recall that Bill Matheson did his library school internship at UCLA.

It is with great affection that I recall Luther Evans. From first meeting I was inspired by his energy, warmth, and democratic ways of administering. If I had to name a single role model, it would be Luther Evans. We kept in touch in our years of retirement and were planning to meet again in San Antonio when death took him.

An unusual connection with the Library of Congress came from Fay's and my having been at our alma mater on September 22, 1941, for the premiere of Benjamin Britten's First String Quartet, commissioned by Elizabeth Sprague Coolidge. The composer and his friend Peter Pears were also there that Sunday afternoon at Occidental

College. Mrs. Coolidge, then living in Oakland, California, was unable to attend. The correspondence between her and Britten, now in the Library's Music Division, concerned with the composition and rehearsals of the quartet, occurred while Britten and Pears were living in Escondido, as guests of the duo pianists Bartlett and Robertson.

That Spanish word means "hidden." As a pacifist, Britten had left Britain to escape the war, and he had settled in that small town inland a few miles from the Pacific. At a bookstore in nearby San Diego he and Pears came upon the decisive volume of George Crabbe's poetry that led to their return to England, the opera *Peter Grimes*, and lasting fame. My hope is to edit those letters, after publication of the official life and letters by Donald Mitchell.

My life has thus been one of many connections with people and books, books and people, many of them of other times. We learned from Carlyle MacIntyre that we live in a cultural continuum in which we are free to move back and forth through the centuries. Books are islands in the ocean of Time. They are also oases in the desert of of Time.

When John Cole invited me here, he suggested that I might want to speak in defense of the book, in what some of the faint-hearted see as an embattled time. I gave it only passing thought. Defend the book? How absurd! To me the book has never been merely a physical object which is sometimes beautiful, though more likely is not. Professor MacIntyre's own library was a pretty beat-up houseful of working copies, bearing his hieroglyphic notes, all doomed to be lost in a great rain and mud slide on New Year's Eve 1933, when not only books but house and everything in it were lost. The book was to him and is to me what Milton said it is: the precious lifeblood of a man treasured up against time. And it is also what MacIntyre said it is: next to mother's milk the best food. Defend lifeblood? Defend mother's milk?

Twenty years ago I left administrative work after it culminated in a new school of librarianship, founded on the belief that books, in whatever form and shape, are not mere artifacts but symbols of truth and vessels of learning. Fourteen years of planning went into that school, years of persistent belief in the need for it, shared by a small group of us and by librarians in the region and beyond.

This national library's contribution was Seymour Lubetzky. He and I began our careers together as juniors at UCLA, and when he left, to spend eighteen years at the Library of Congress as the mastermind of cataloging and classification, we vowed to come back to UCLA together when the new school was ready to open. And so it came to pass.

Frances Clarke Sayers and Andrew Horn too came back to our first faculty, from the New York Public

Library and the University of North Carolina. And later there joined us the UCLA alumnus who eventually succeeded Horn, as Horn succeeded me, as dean. He was the humanistic mathematician Robert M. Hayes. As early as 1959 I sensed that our future lay in his hands. And that too came to pass. Gradually lured from industry, first with a campus parking permit and finally with a professorship, Bob Hayes proved the one to lead the school—and librarianship—in the refinement and uses of information science.

Two decades ago, when I knew that I had done all I could do to effect change, I retired and left the school with Horn and Hayes and their colleagues. No longer was I the right person at the right place at the right time. Now that I have retired again, and I trust for the last time, I hope to adapt to it. I might even catch up on my reading. For instance, there's *War and Peace.*

Do I sound mellowed? If one lives long enough those rough edges do get smoothed. Although reconciled to change, I am troubled by what I see of library schools teaching the new technology at the expense of our need for more than information. Who will prepare librarians to serve children, young people, middle-aged dreamers, and old folks? The responsibility belongs to the teacher, not the administrator. And remember what Bishop Grundtvig said, that *who* teaches is more important than *what* is taught. If that Danish educational reformer is not authority enough, then listen to our own great spokesman: "Who you are stands behind you," Emerson said, "and thunders so loudly, I cannot hear what you say."

Technology changes, formats change; lifeblood and mother's milk do not. Although how we search for truth and how we apply what we find is always in flux, our need for joy and security and solace is constant. Are not today's marvels of library operation—call it housekeeping—only a new level of efficiency?

Though the configuration of the night sky moves through its phases, its governing laws are unalterable. When we look up at night, we see what the Greeks saw. Their pain is our pain. Hear how Mary Barnard rendered that immortal Sapphic cry:

> Tonight I've watched the moon
>   And then the Pleiades go down,
> The night is now half-gone.
>   Youth goes. I am in bed alone.

From this high launching pad, let me descend with a few final words to round the circle that brought me back to the banks of the Potomac.

We once lived here on Park Road. The house is still there—at least it was twenty years ago, the last time I was here. It stood on a high embankment leading down to Rock Creek Park. On Sunday mornings during my childhood, before we moved west to stay, along would come riding on a white horse, a man who raised in his stirrups and doffed his hat to us children and our elders, who stood on the high ground and waved back—to our president, Theodore Roosevelt.

About that same time, on May 23, 1910, after a period of unbroken overcast, my mother wrote in her journal: "Cleared at night and we saw the comet—Halley's—at last. The tail too, tho it was dim owing to moonlight." My earliest memory is of a night soon thereafter of her waking me, age four, and carrying me to the high window. There in the sky I too saw it—the shining head, the streaming tail.

Now we have returned together, the comet and I, but not to stay. Halley's will be leaving soon and won't be back for another seventy-six years. Fay and I, too, are leaving for our home on the desert, and I don't know if we'll ever be back. I guess you'll have to come our way if we are to meet again.

And so, thanks for a wonderful visit—and good night.

This booklet was designed by Ward Ritchie and printed in an edition of 2,000 copies by Richard Hoffman in Van Nuys, California. The type used is Weiss, the paper is acid-free Mohawk Superfine, and the cover is sky- blue Sundance.